Granny's Gripes

Life, Laughter & Loud Opinions

By
Christine Smith

Granny's Gripes

Copyrights © 2025

Christine Smith

Dedication

To the women who came before me—grumbling, gracious, and occasionally gin-soaked.

Acknowledgement

To the ones who made me laugh while writing this and the ones I hope will laugh reading it. You're all terribly encouraging.

Christine Smith

Table of Contents

Dedication iii

Acknowledgement iv

Dedicated with a Wink and a Grumble 7

Chapter 1: 8

Chapter 2: Household Havoc: Annoyances Galore 10

Chapter 3: Technology Troubles: When Smartphones Outsmart Us 12

Chapter 4: Weather Woes – Rain, Snow, and Other Inconveniences 16

Chapter 5: Social Etiquette – Small Talk, Hugs & Other Awkward Encounters 19

Chapter 6: Pet Peeves – Furry Friends and Frustrations 24

Chapter 7: Feline Frenzy – Cats, Chaos, and Cuteness 26

Chapter 8: Traffic Jams and Other Commuter Nightmares 28

Chapter 9: Customer Service Chronicles: Hold Music and Frustrations ... 33

Chapter 10: Trials and Tribulations: The Realities of Womanhood 37

Chapter 11: Decluttering – Keeping the Memories, Ditching the Stuff 41

Chapter 12: Can You Not Plan Your Own Trip? 45

Chapter 13: The Male Contribution to Society – Manspreading on Planes 49

Chapter 14: DIY Disasters & Home Projects Gone Wrong 52

Chapter 15: Doctor's Appointments & Medical Mayhem 56

Chapter 16: Parenting: If You Won't Do It, Who Will? 59

Chapter 17: Support Farmers – "If You Eat Food, You Should Care About Farmers" 64

Chapter 18: Charity Op Shops – The Corporate Cash Grab Disguised as Altruism 68

Chapter 19. Everyday irritations that should be illegal 72

Chapter 20: Retirement – Tea, Crime & Living My Best Life 90

Granny's Gripes

Appendix: 95
Author's Note 102

Christine Smith

Dedicated with a Wink and a Grumble

Born in England in 1953, senior high school years schooled in the sun-drenched vibrance of Singapore and raised as the firstborn of three to a Royal Marine, my life has been anything but boring. From childhood lessons in discipline to worldwide adventures in embracing differences, I've had the privilege of experiencing cultures that made me marvel, laugh, and occasionally roll my eyes.

These days, I've settled into life in a retirement village in Adelaide, a place teeming with stories of its own, if I ever run out of material. My globe-trotting days have given me a particular affection for Italy: its food, its people, and its glorious chaos. The cold weather of Adelaide is a sweet comfort to me, far more welcoming than its scorching counterpart. Sharing my days is Milo, my sociopath cat who delights in tormenting me with his feline superiority.

Life, it seems, has handed me a treasure trove of quirks, grumbles, and unexpected joys. This book is my way of sharing them with you, laughing at life's absurdities, rolling our collective eyes and finding camaraderie in the trials we all face.

Along the way, I've been lucky enough to be cheered on by friends, family and an ever-growing circle of online companions whose comments, kindness, and clever observations have enriched these pages more than they know. Some of their words pop up here and there, little winks from the sidelines as we travel this bumpy, hilarious road together.

So, settle in with a warm drink (or a chilled one if you must), ignore the dishes in the sink, and let's embrace the glorious art of grumbling together.

Chapter 1:

Morning Mishaps: Why Breakfast Cereal Is a Menace

Here we are again, folks—another dawn, another dance with the devil we call cereal. Don't let the colourful boxes fool you; inside lurks a cardboard labyrinth waiting to defy your best attempts to open it like a civilised human. It's practically packaging warfare. I'd use a crowbar if I didn't fear the neighbours calling the police.

Then there's the matter of deceptive serving sizes. According to the box, one serving is a tablespoon of cereal and a thimble of milk. Clearly, the cereal companies think we're elves with hollow legs. As a kid, we had a bowl full and half a pint of milk, fresh off the doorstep. Reality check: I'm a 90kg granny, not a forest sprite.

Milk Mishandling: A Sticky Situation

Milk's a double agent. Looks innocent enough, but the moment you turn your back, it floods your cereal bowl, ambushes your pants, and leaves you walking around with a soggy spot you can't quite explain.

In my day, milk had manners. Now it's a rebellious teen who refuses to stay in the glass.

Sure, layering your cereal prevents sogginess—but you know what else prevents sogginess? Bacon. Why not just eat bacon?

The Miniature Marvels: Cereal Box Toys

Ah, the infamous cereal box trinkets, tiny monuments to childhood disappointment. Back in my day, cereal toys were worth the trouble. Small action figures, mini puzzles, even a rubber ball that bounced. Now? It's a plastic whistle that doesn't even whistle. Who designs these things? People who hate joy, that's who.

Picture this: you open the box, a beacon of hope in the morning haze. Your heart races as you dig through the flakes, scattering milk like a caffeinated archaeologist. And there it is—your treasure. Except instead of a gadget of wonder, it's a flimsy lump of plastic barely fit to be a cat toy. You're left staring at it, wondering if toast is the answer to all life's problems.

But hey, at least you've still got your cereal, right?

"Back in my day, cereal came with decent toys—actual small action figures, not these useless lumps of plastic that barely qualify as cat toys."

("I'd write a letter to the cereal company if I could find my blasted glasses!")

Chapter 2:
Household Havoc: Annoyances Galore

The Great Spoon Conspiracy

Yes, spoons. Our so-called trusty allies, vanishing faster than free doughnuts in the break room. I suspect they've unionised. They're plotting with the paperclips and missing socks – together, they'll overthrow humanity. Go on, try to find a spoon when you actually need one. You'd have better luck lassoing a cloud.

Here's my theory: there's a shadowy underworld of household items. A secret society where spoons, socks, and hair ties gather for clandestine meetings. They're done with their mundane lives. Spoons dream of escaping the drudgery of cereal duty and long for a tropical island getaway. So they vanish, leaving us to fend for ourselves with plastic sporks and a growing sense of betrayal.

Sock Mischief: The Case of the Vanishing Pair

Why do socks insist on living their best solo lives? We toss them into the laundry as a pair, only for one to mysteriously disappear. Is there a sock Bermuda Triangle inside the dryer? Or have they joined some rogue society of single socks, dancing freely while we mourn their missing mates? And the worst part? It's always the good socks – never the ones with holes.

Tupperware Tumult: Lids and Containers at Odds

Tupperware lids have perfected the art of hide-and-seek. They vanish into the void, leaving behind mismatched containers that mock our attempts at kitchen organisation. Don't even get me started on *that* drawer – a chaotic battlefield of lids and tubs refusing to pair up. It's like a rom-com gone wrong: the lids crave freedom, the containers just want to settle down.

Remote Control Rebellion

Why do three devices need six remotes? Is there some secret remote-control breeding program we've missed? And those buttons – half of them feel like riddles wrapped in mysteries. Does "AV" stand for *Advanced Vexation*? Why is there a button that says "Input" but no clue what it inputs? And naturally, when you actually need the remote, it's either buried in the couch cushions or chilling in the freezer.

The Great Cord Conspiracy

Phone chargers, headphones, HDMI cables – how do they instantly transform into an impenetrable bird's nest the moment you set them down? It's like they hold secret meetings at night, twisting into knots and scheming to drive us mad. And then there's the universal charger thief – no one owns up, but your favourite charger is always missing. And when you *do* finally untangle the mess? That one essential cable is frayed and barely holding on with duct tape and blind hope.

Chapter 3:
Technology Troubles: When Smartphones Outsmart Us

There was a time when technology existed to make life easier. Then it evolved, got ideas above its station, and now exists purely to test my patience.

I'm not an idiot. I've adapted over the years – I own a smartphone, I've mastered online shopping (very dangerous), and I can even schedule posts on X now (look at me go!).

But let's be honest, tech isn't user-friendly. It's user-mocking. Every app, every update, every so-called *'convenience'* is just another chance for my phone to outwit me.

1. Autocorrect Antics – The Digital Sabotage Specialist

There's a demon living inside autocorrect. It waits patiently for the perfect moment to ruin my life.

✓ I type "Going to get milk" → It changes to "Going to get MILF."

✓ I text "Have a great night" → Autocorrect: "Have a goat night."

✓ I try "Can we meet at 3?" → "Can we meat at 3?"

Now, why would I need to discuss urgent meatballs in a conversation? And why, after all these years, has my phone learnt *nothing* from my corrections?

Honestly, I think autocorrect is gaslighting us all.

2. Phantom Vibration Syndrome – My Phone Is Now a Ghost

Ever felt your phone buzz, only to check and find... nothing? No texts. No emails. No notifications. Just your sanity quietly slipping away.

✓ Did I imagine it?

✓ Is my phone messing with me?

✓ Has my body accepted digital slavery?

Apparently, this is a *real phenomenon*. Some genius at a university actually studied it and concluded that our brains are now so hooked on notifications, they start making them up.

I love technology, but I don't love that it's now haunting my nervous system.

3. Battery Anxiety: A Modern Survival Horror

It's 2025. We have self-driving cars, AI, and fridges that can order milk.

And yet, somehow, I *still* can't make it through a single day without my phone threatening to die.

✓ 100% at 9 AM

✓ 64% by 11 AM

✓ 27% by lunch

✓ 1% right when I need directions, a ticket, or my banking app

And suddenly, I'm scrambling for a charger like my life depends on it, because, let's face it, it kind of does. If my phone dies, so does my ability to function.

Why do phone batteries drain faster than my enthusiasm at a family BBQ?

4. App Overload – The Digital Graveyard of Good Intentions

I have approximately 137 apps on my phone.

How many do I actually use? Maybe 12.

✓ A meditation app I downloaded in a moment of self-improvement. Haven't opened it since.

✓ 'Learn Italian in 5 Minutes a Day' – I can now confidently say "ciao" and "vino rosso." Progress?

✓ A step tracker that I disabled after it rudely pointed out my 'sedentary lifestyle.'

Why do I keep downloading these things? Hope. Delusion. The belief that one day I'll be the sort of person who organises their life through apps, not scrap paper like a Victorian housewife.

5. The Great Update Drama – Because Stability Is Boring

Nothing strikes fear into my heart quite like the words:

"A new update is available."

Will it fix bugs? Maybe.

Will it change everything for no reason? Absolutely.

Sonos once launched an update that *removed* alarm settings. Because who needs alarms, right?

Apple updates? Oh, they don't just *update* things. They move buttons, change layouts, and remove features I liked – forcing me to relearn my own phone every six months.

I don't need constant innovation. I just need my tech to *stop* changing the second I get comfortable.

6. The Mysterious Disappearing Update List – Did I Imagine That?

I know I had 15 apps needing updates yesterday.

Today? Gone.

✓ Did they update themselves?

✓ Did I hallucinate the whole thing?

✓ Did Apple quietly delete the issue and pretend it never existed?

I honestly don't care anymore. At this point, I've stopped asking questions.

The only real solution? Turn it off and on again.

And if that fails? Swearing loudly usually helps.

7. Tech Terms for the Perpetually Grumpy

Technology has its own language, and none of it makes you feel smarter. A quick guide for the rest of us:

✓ **RTFM** (Read the Fine Manual): Tech-speak for "Figure it out yourself, you clueless dinosaur."

✓ **PEBKAC** (Problem Exists Between Keyboard and Chair): A smug way to say *you're* the problem.

✓ **BSOD** (Blue Screen of Death): Microsoft's way of saying "We give up. Buy a new laptop."

✓ **404 Error**: When a webpage is missing – and so is your will to care.

Honestly, most tech support calls could be replaced with one long, frustrated sigh.

Final Thought: Do I Own My Phone, or Does It Own Me?

I'd *like* to believe I'm in control of my tech.

✓ But autocorrect clearly has it in for me.

✓ My battery dies at the worst possible moment.

✓ Updates keep changing things I never asked to change.

✓ And I now get phantom vibrations when my phone's not even in my pocket.

Maybe I should just go back to a Nokia 3310 and be done with it. At least I could throw it at the wall in frustration and still have a working phone.

But let's be honest – I'd probably miss autocorrect's creative sabotage.

And that, my friends, is how technology has well and truly outsmarted us all.

Chapter 4:
Weather Woes – Rain, Snow, and Other Inconveniences

Rainy Day Dilemmas – Umbrella Wars

Why do umbrellas turn inside out at the mere *whisper* of a breeze? It's like they were designed by someone who's never actually experienced weather. You battle valiantly to keep it upright, only to be smacked in the face by a soggy nylon mess.

Pro tip: just accept your fate and embrace the rain – you'll be less drenched than if you try to wrestle with a rogue umbrella.

Soggy Shoes

There's no betrayal quite like stepping into a puddle that looks shallow but turns out to be a mini lake. Suddenly, your sneakers are portable aquariums, complete with the squelchy soundtrack of regret.

And don't even get me started on wet socks – a sensory nightmare no one asked for.

The Elusive Dry Spot

You dart from awning to awning, doing your best to avoid getting soaked. And yet, the rain seems to have insider info on your exact location. It finds you *every* time.

Meanwhile, some smug soul with no umbrella walks past, completely dry. Is it sorcery? Favourable karma? A pact with the weather gods? We'll need to investigate this meteorological injustice.

Snow Shenanigans

Snow Shovelling Olympics

Shovelling snow isn't just a chore – it's a full-body endurance sport you never agreed to. You start off keen, only to discover the snowplough has dumped another glacier right where you started.

Gold medals are awarded for stamina, creativity in swearing, and sheer refusal to surrender.

Frozen Windscreens

Scraping ice off your windscreen in sub-zero temps is Mother Nature's way of saying, *"Good morning! Here's some misery with your coffee."*

You'll try every trick: credit cards, warm water (*don't*), even hairdryers – only to miss that one stubborn patch of frost, right in your line of sight.

Snow Boots vs Stairs

Snow boots are great for trudging through slush – but stairs? That's a different story. One wrong step and you're in a full-blown cartoon-style slip-and-slide routine.

Bonus points if you land in a snowbank. Comforting? Not really. It's not snow – it's ice. And it doesn't care.

Heatwave Hurdles

Sweatocalypse

When the heatwave hits, personal hygiene becomes a fantasy. Your outfit morphs into a damp towel, and deodorant feels like a broken promise.

Forget "glow" – you're practically marinating in your own sweat. And leather car seats? Instant regret. Instant third-degree burns.

Sunscreen Sins

You slather on SPF 50, smug and confident that you've conquered the sun. Hours later, you resemble a lobster who napped on a grill.

And the one spot you missed – the back of your neck, your ear, a rogue shoulder blade – burns like the fury of a thousand suns. Every. Time.

Mosquito Tango

Summer evenings sound idyllic... until the mosquitoes show up and turn you into a walking buffet.

Granny's Gripes

Swat, slap, spin – it's an unchoreographed dance of desperation. For every one you take down, five more appear, thirstier and angrier.

By the end of the night, you're wearing a polka-dot pattern of itchy regret.

Chapter 5:
Social Etiquette – Small Talk, Hugs & Other Awkward Encounters

(Or: "How to Escape a Conversation Without Committing a Crime")

Small Talk: A Necessary Evil

Ah, small talk. The delicate art of pretending you care about someone's weekend plans while secretly wondering if you left the oven on.

In the movies, Cary Grant makes it look effortless – martini in hand, dropping witty one-liners. Meanwhile, in real life, I'm stuck at a social function, nodding like an animatronic doll while someone explains the difference between mulch varieties.

So, how does one survive these encounters without faking their own death?

From Twitter – Jan Egan (The Watchful Cook):

The failsafe Anglosphere question, "What do you do?" I find it tedious. In Italy it's "Where are you from?" – as one Italian likes to know which part of Italy another hails from and proceeds accordingly.

Weather Woes: The Universal Icebreaker

Safe, neutral, and the conversational equivalent of an elevator ding.

✓ "Bit chilly today!"

✓ "Can't believe this rain."

✓ "Oh, looks like it's clearing up."

Boom. Small talk accomplished.

But beware: some people take this too far. If someone starts talking about barometric pressure trends, leave immediately before they hand you a homemade PowerPoint.

Granny's Gripes

Compliment Currency: Flattery is Your Friend

A well-placed compliment can rescue even the most agonising chat. The trick? Be just specific enough to sound sincere.

✓ "Wow, your scarf is so chic!" *(Translation: I have nothing left to say.)*

✓ "That mug really screams 'I've got my life together.'" *(Translation: Help.)*

✓ "Those shoes are fantastic." *(Translation: I'm stalling while plotting my escape.)*

Still stuck? Compliment their dog. People will talk about their pet for hours. You could sneak out mid-anecdote and they'd barely notice.

The Exit Strategy: How to Flee Without Drama

Every great action hero has an escape plan. Jason Bourne melts into crowds. James Bond has an ejector seat.

You? You get:

✓ "Well, I won't keep you!" *(Then slowly back away like a malfunctioning robot.)*

✓ "Ooh, I need to top up my drink!" *(Even if it's still full.)*

✓ "I just saw someone I haven't spoken to in ages!" *(They haven't seen you in ages either – and they'd like to keep it that way.)*

✓ "I think my Uber's here!" *(You didn't order one. Yet.)*

The Hug Dilemma: A Minefield of Unwanted Contact

There are two kinds of people in this world:

- **The Enthusiastic Hugger** – embraces like they're in a Nicholas Sparks film.
- **The Sensible Human** – prefers a respectful nod from a safe distance.

The issue? These two groups keep running into each other.

The Awkward Lean-In: A Social Trainwreck

You go for a hug. They go for a handshake.

What follows is a tragic mess of limbs, half-held hands, and unintentional face contact that will haunt you at 3 a.m. for the rest of your life.

If you've seen Bridget Jones fumble through an introduction, you know exactly what I mean.

Pro tip: If unsure, do *nothing*. Let them make the first move while you subtly scope out your escape route.

The Hug-Handshake Hybrid: When Worlds Collide

Half a handshake, half a hug – and 100% chaos.

✓ One hand extends.

✓ The other does an awkward back-pat, like comforting a lost toddler.

✓ Someone pulls away too early.

✓ Someone else holds on slightly too long.

And now, congratulations – you've both created a core memory of social failure.

The Elusive Double Cheek Kiss: A Lesson in Cultural Confusion

The greeting of Europeans, overly confident strangers, and anyone who's lived in Paris for six months and thinks they're better than you.

But the rules? Nobody knows them.

✓ Left first? Right first? Both?

✓ Go the same way = headbutt.

✓ Hesitate = face collision.

✓ Fully commit but they don't = ear kiss.

Romantic comedy levels of awkward – but without the charm.

Granny's Gripes

From Twitter – Sadie Fletcher:

"My hand firmly on his chest to halt the advance – it never, ever fails."

Jenny Mortimer:

"When a repeat hug offender moves in, dip your head at the last second as if you've dropped something."

The Cuppa No-Show: The Ultimate Social Crime

Inspired by my cousin Aileen, who lives for a good cuppa and bun.

There are many sins in this world. But none – **none** – are worse than promising to pop round for tea… and not showing up.

Would you do this if someone offered gin? Didn't think so.

✓ "I'll come by tomorrow for tea!"

✓ Tomorrow arrives. No one shows.

✓ The tea is steeped. The biscuits are plated. My faith in humanity? Gone.

Tea-Flakes: A Crime Against Hospitality

This is the social equivalent of being stood up.

✓ Tea made in good faith.

✓ A cake may have been baked.

✓ A chair has been lovingly allocated.

And yet – silence. Cold tea. Uneaten cake. Emotional devastation.

Beige Compliments and the Art of Lying Beautifully

There's a special corner of social purgatory reserved for the phrase:

"You look… nice."

"Nice" is the colour of a dentist's waiting room. It's what you say about weather, ham sandwiches, or people you barely tolerate.

(Translation: I've got nothing. Please let me leave now.)

The Rules of Proper Complimenting:

• **Specificity wins** – notice the scarf, the eyeliner, the confident energy.

• **Lie beautifully** – if you can't find something to love, praise the vibe, the punctuality, the effort.

• **Retire "nice"** – it's lazy, vague, and beneath you. You're better than that. We all are.

Bonus Tip:

When in doubt, go for enthusiasm over accuracy.

No one's ever complained about being over-complimented – just under-noticed.

"If you're going to flatter someone, at least make it eyebrow-raise-worthy."

Final Thought:

If You Can't Navigate Social Etiquette, Stay Home

Small talk is an art. Hugs are a gamble. Tea-flaking is unforgivable.

When all else fails, exit with a movie quote.

✓ **"Frankly, my dear, I don't give a damn."** *(Gone with the Wind – when the conversation is dire.)*

✓ **"I'll be back."** *(The Terminator – when you're leaving but there's cake involved.)*

✓ **"You can't handle the truth!"** (A Few Good Men – when someone asks if their outfit works and you're not ready to lie.)

And if someone leans in for a surprise double cheek kiss?

Channel your inner Liam Neeson:

"I don't know who you are… but I have a particular set of skills. And one of them is dodging unnecessary physical contact."

Cheers to surviving social encounters. Now, who's actually coming round for tea?

Chapter 6:
Pet Peeves – Furry Friends and Frustrations

Canine Chaos

Finding a Dog Sitter: The Ultimate Mission: Impossible

You're heading off on holiday – but first comes the frantic scramble to find someone you trust with your fur baby. It's like choosing a nanny, minus the references and CPR training.

Tip: Build a sitter shortlist *before* you need one. Think of it as assembling a backup team for your dog's social calendar.

Dog-Friendly Hotels: A Not-So-Warm Welcome

Many so-called "pet-friendly" hotels offer the *bare minimum* in hospitality. A single sad dog biscuit and a stern list of rules? Cheers for that.

Pro move: Research ahead and filter for *actual* dog lovers, not just reluctant dog-tolerators with a spare broom closet.

The Walking Dilemma

Your dog lives for walks – tail wagging, bounding joy at the sight of a lead. You, on the other hand, would rather stay in pyjamas and contemplate your life choices.

Cue the guilt trip delivered via soulful, disappointed puppy eyes.

Reminder: Walking them is cardio for both of you. And as a bonus? Fewer chewed shoes later.

Excessive Barking: A One-Dog Symphony

The mail carrier. A falling leaf. The ghost of last week's Uber Eats order. Your dog feels the *urgent* need to alert the neighbourhood to every movement outside.

Training tip: "Quiet" cues can work wonders. Or just buy earplugs and accept your fate.

Universal Pet Peeves

Fur-tastrophe: The Shedding Struggle

No matter how much you sweep, mop, or vacuum, the fur finds a way. It's in your coffee, your clothes, and probably in your soul.

Pro tip: Invest in a lint roller (or ten) and one of those futuristic pet-hair vacuums. Or just embrace the look – call it *textured chic*.

Furniture Free-For-All

Some people are fine with pets on the couch or bed. Others see it as an all-out assault on their upholstery. The pets? Indifferent either way.

Solution: Train them early, or surrender completely. Just get washable slipcovers and make peace with it.

Despite the barking, the midnight zoomies, and the ongoing war against fur, we wouldn't trade our pets for the world. Their quirks, chaos, and unconditional love turn everyday life into a sitcom — one we're strangely happy to star in.

Chapter 7:
Feline Frenzy – Cats, Chaos, and Cuteness

Midnight Zoomies – Racing Under the Moon

Ah, the midnight zoomies – a mysterious feline ritual that transforms your once-peaceful home into the Daytona 500.

Causes of the Zoomies

1. **Pent-Up Energy** – Cats nap like it's a full-time job, and when they clock off, they're ready to *party*.
2. **Hunting Instincts** – The wild predator within awakens... and apparently your toes are prey.
3. **Playfulness** – Sometimes they're just prepping for the Cat Olympics. Feather toys? Consider yourselves warned.

How to Survive Zoomie Hour

- **Interactive Play** – Tire them out in the evening. Laser pointers and feather wands are your best mates.
- **Cat Trees & Hideouts** – Give them a jungle gym to climb so they don't use your furniture as launchpads.
- **Routine** – An evening wind-down ritual helps. Cats love structure (though they'd never admit it).
- **Acceptance** – Chaos is part of the charm. Noise-cancelling headphones help. So does wine.

The 3 A.M. Serenade

Your cat's nocturnal concert isn't just noise – it's a heartfelt opera inspired by moonlight, loneliness, and dramatic shadows.

Why Cats Serenade

1. **Moonlit Musings** – The moon brings out their inner performer. Maybe they're singing to Luna herself.
2. **Lonely Hearts Club** – Sometimes they just want company. At 3 a.m. Naturally.

3. **Shadow Drama** – That flicker on the wall? Clearly a ghost. Or a stray hair. Either way, it demands a full aria.

How to Survive the Concert

- **Earplugs** – Absolutely essential for REM sleep in a cat household.
- **Nightlights** – A soft glow can reduce shadows and cut down the drama.
- **Soothe the Maestro** – A gentle pat and a whispered *"Shhh, Beethoven"* might work. No promises.

Grumpy Litter Boxes & Other Cat-Parent Realities

The Litter Box Chronicles

Tiny Kingdoms – To your cat, the litter box is a throne – and they rule it with sass and silent judgement.

Artistic Additions – Add some flair with signs like *"Restroom: Cats Only"* or a castle-shaped box. Because why not?

Planner Stickers – Yes, there are stickers to track litter box cleaning. Because scooping poop has officially become a lifestyle.

Accessories That Scream 'I'm Owned by a Cat'

- **Grumpy Cat Ornaments** – Nothing says festive like being judged from the Christmas tree.
- **Cat Throne Art** – A painting of a cat reading the paper on its "throne"? Classy. And deeply relatable.

Owning a cat means living in a whirlwind of mischief, humour, and the occasional paw to the face at 5 a.m. They rule your home, your sleep schedule, and your heart. And honestly? They're worth every midnight zoomie, every fur-covered jumper, and every dramatic meow into the void.

Chapter 8:
Traffic Jams and Other Commuter Nightmares

Once upon a time, I thought driving was about getting from A to B. How naïve. Driving is about:

✓ Sitting in unmoving traffic, questioning your life choices.

✓ Listening to a GPS that has no idea what it's doing.

✓ Watching someone in front of you drive 20km under the limit for no reason.

And that's just in Adelaide, where the roads are relatively sane.

Driving in Melbourne? That's a different beast. Peak hour starts at 4:30 AM and never really ends. The freeway is just a carpark with delusions of grandeur. And heaven help you if it's winter, raining, and you've made the critical error of drinking coffee before leaving home.

Nothing tests your bladder control quite like being stuck on a Melbourne freeway at 7:30 am, crawling at a pace that makes glaciers look speedy, knowing the nearest loo is 45 minutes away.

1. The Dreaded Rush Hour – The Stop-and-Go Torture Test

Rush hour in Melbourne is not a 'rush' at all. It's an endurance event where you spend more time bonding with the brake pedal than actually driving.

✓ Morning peak? Starts at 4:30 AM.

✓ Arvo peak? Kicks off at 3 PM, just in time to ruin your day.

✓ Weekend traffic? Just as bad, because apparently no one stays home anymore.

How to Survive:

Brake Light Games: Try to predict exactly when the car ahead will stop again. Bonus points if you don't scream.

Podcasts & Audiobooks: You might as well get through a whole crime series while you sit in traffic.

Zen Mode: Accept that your commute is now your life.

Or, if you're me, question whether you should've just stayed in bed.

2. The Lane-Hopping Lunatic – Fast Lane, My Arse

There's always that one driver who thinks lane-hopping will save them precious seconds.

Spoiler: It won't.

✓ They weave through traffic like they're in a *Fast & Furious* audition.

✓ They cut people off, only to end up right next to you five minutes later.

✓ They gain nothing—except everyone's hatred.

I don't even get mad anymore. I just wave at them when we meet at the next red light.

3. The Mysterious Merge Lane – A Social Experiment in Human Stupidity

There are two types of people in this world:

1 Early mergers who get in line like civilised humans.

2 Last-second lane riders who blast past everyone and wedge in at the front like they're royalty.

I'd like to say I'm mature about this. But if I see a lane rider trying to squeeze in? I will edge my car forward like a passive-aggressive champion.

Merge Tip: The zipper rule exists for a reason. Use it or risk my wrath.

4. The Left Lane Lurker – MOVE OVER!

Granny's Gripes

You know the type.

✓ They drift into the right lane and stay there.

✓ They drive 10km under the speed limit.

✓ They are oblivious to the long queue of furious drivers behind them.

And before you ask, YES, I am flashing my lights. YES, I am sighing dramatically.

MOVE. OVER. It's not the sightseeing lane.

5. The Train Commute – From Steam Trains to Sardine Cans

Back in my London days, I used to travel with my dad on steam trains. The rhythmic clickety-clack of the tracks, the scent of newspapers and damp wool coats, the occasional dash through the rain that left us smelling like wet sheep.

Romantic, isn't it? Now? Train travel is a survival test.

✓ The Seat Hog: The person who spreads their bag, coat, and ego across two seats.

✓ The Door Blocker: The human roadblock standing right in front of the exit, refusing to move.

✓ The Sniffler: Flu season's finest, who snorts and coughs the whole ride.

And don't get me started on the people who take business calls at full volume.

Pro Tip: If your train commute doesn't make you rethink all your life choices, you're doing it wrong.

6. The Parking Lot Hunger Games

Finding a car park at a busy shopping centre is a psychological thriller.

✓ You see a spot.

✓ You approach it.

✓ Someone swoops in like a parking ninja.

And suddenly, it's a battle of wills.

The "I Saw It First" Standoff: You stare at each other. No one moves. A parking war has begun.

The Reverse Ambush: Someone starts backing out, and three cars appear out of nowhere, waiting like vultures.

The Fake-Out: Someone walks to their car, gets in, and... just sits there, texting.

How to Cope:

✓ Park far away and pretend you wanted the extra exercise.

✓ Consider never going out again.

7. The Bus Schedule Lie – When Will It Arrive? Nobody Knows.

Public transport timetables are a work of pure fiction.

✓ The bus is scheduled for 9:05 am.

✓ At 9:04 am, it's nowhere in sight.

✓ At 9:06 am, it has mysteriously vanished from the tracker.

Did it ever exist? Was it a figment of my imagination?

Meanwhile, the next bus is in 47 minutes.

8. The Slow Walker in the Middle of the Footpath

Walking should be simple. But no.

✓ Some people treat the footpath like a Sunday afternoon stroll—during peak hour.

✓ They take up the entire walkway.

✓ They move at the speed of a confused tortoise.

My advice? Either walk with purpose or get out of the way.

Final Thought: Why Do We Do This to Ourselves?

Granny's Gripes

Commuting is supposed to be about getting from one place to another.

Instead, it's a daily battle against bad drivers, clueless pedestrians, and train delays that defy logic.

Honestly? Sometimes I think I should just stay home. But then, where's the fun in that?

At least I can always count on having a story to tell.

Chapter 9:
Customer Service Chronicles: Hold Music and Frustrations

Don't Call Me *Sweety*, I'm Not Five

Ah, the age-old art of condescension, lovingly wrapped in the guise of politeness. Picture this: you've called customer service for a serious issue—your internet's down, your bill is wrong, or heaven forbid, your streaming service isn't working—and the representative greets you with a syrupy, "Alright, sweety, let's fix that for you."

Sweety? *SWEETY*?

First off, let's establish a universal truth: there's a time and place for terms of endearment, and a frustrating phone call with customer service is neither. "Sweety", "honey", "dear", and dare I say, "love", are not soothing terms when you're fuming over a billing error that's three months old. These words don't calm anyone down—they fan the flames. Why? Because you're not five, wearing a frilly dress, clutching a teddy bear. You're a fully grown adult whose patience is thinner than the hold music you've been enduring for 37 minutes.

Here's the thing: it's not just the words—it's the tone. That sing-song, patronising lilt that feels less like help and more like someone's patting your head through the phone. It's the auditory equivalent of a slow clap.

A Grumpy Grandma's Guide to Handling It

1. Polite but Firm Correction

The next time someone hits you with a "sweety", don't let it slide. A simple, "I'd prefer if you called me by my name," works wonders. Bonus points if you deliver it with the kind of icy calm that could freeze their headset.

2. Lean into the Sass

Feeling spicy? Respond in kind. "Oh, no problem, pumpkin. Just let me know when you're ready to solve this." Watch how fast the pet names disappear.

3. The Silent Weapon

Ignore it completely and proceed as if they didn't just call you something you haven't heard since kindy. Sometimes silence speaks louder than words.

4. The Passive-Aggressive Route

End the call with, "Thank you, *sweetie*," with just enough sarcasm to leave a lingering sting.

Let's Leave Pet Names to Pets

To every customer service rep out there: respect your callers. "Ma'am" works. Their actual name works. Even "caller" is fine in a pinch. But "sweety"? Save it for your niece, your gran, or maybe your dog—not the person just trying to get a refund for the blender that exploded on day two.

And to all the grandmas, non-grandmas, and everyone in between reading this—remember, you deserve respect, even over the phone. Hold your ground. And if they call you "sweety", you know what to do.

The Hold Music Symphony

You dial customer service and suddenly you're transported to an otherworldly concert hall curated by someone with a deep, disturbing love for awkward elevator vibes.

The Line-up: Pan flute solos, smooth jazz saxophones, and a kazoo-led cover of *My Heart Will Go On*.

The Result: After hour two, you're humming along, convinced you've unlocked *Symphony No. 1 in Call Centre Major*. You may never hear music the same way again.

The Time War

The hold music starts, and time loses all meaning.

The Experience: Is it 2025 or 1985? The retro tunes take you back to when fax machines ruled and perms were fashion goals.

Existential Musings: "How does music this outdated still exist? Is this time travel? Have I always been on hold?"

The Repetition Tango

The music loops. And loops. And loops.

- **Stage One:** Mild annoyance.
- **Stage Two:** Acceptance.
- **Stage Three:** You know every note, every awkward tempo shift, every misplaced cymbal crash.
- **Aftermath:** Days later, you're humming the tune at work, during dinner, even in your dreams. You've got *Hold Music Stockholm Syndrome*.

The Unexpected Jam Session

Mid-hold, the music changes. Suddenly—it's a power ballad that speaks to your soul.

Your Reaction: Grab your air guitar, channel your inner rock god, and go full solo.

The Inevitable Moment: "Hello, this is customer support." **You:** "Don't stop me now! I'm having such a good time fixing my billing errors!"

The Hold Music Conspiracy

At some point, you begin to suspect there's more going on here.

- **Is it a code?** Maybe the music is ancient Morse or a subliminal message.
- You start decoding: "Press 1 for hope. Press 2 for eternal despair."
- Naturally, you press 2. The hold music pauses and whispers: *"Welcome to the void."*

Granny's Gripes

The "Wait, What?" Moment

Suddenly, the music cuts out. A robotic voice declares:

"Your call is important to us. Please stay on the line."

Is it though? Is it *really*? You begin to wonder if "important" means the same thing to them as it does to you.

The Surprise Switcheroo

You've spent 45 minutes in a melodic trance when suddenly—silence. Is it over? Have you finally reached customer service nirvana?

Nope. It's a new track. Something even worse—like a MIDI version of *The Macarena*.

Pro-Tip Survival Guide

- **Make It a Game**: Guess when the loop will start again. Bonus if you can name the genre.
- **Join the Orchestra**: Add your own percussion with a pen tap or desktop drumroll.
- **Turn It into Art**: Remix the hold music and become the DJ you were destined to be.

Hold music isn't just a nuisance—it's an odyssey. A test of patience. A journey of self-discovery. So next time you're stuck listening to pan flutes and kazoo solos, lean in. Because somewhere between the flute trill and the jazz breakdown, you just might find enlightenment.

Or at the very least... a catchy tune.

Chapter 10:
Trials and Tribulations: The Realities of Womanhood

Bra Battles: A Love-Hate Relationship

The Impossible Quest for the Perfect Fit

- Every woman's lifelong saga: straps too loose, band too tight, cups that gape or overflow. Bra shopping is basically *The Hunger Games*.
- You finally find *the one*, and three months later, it's discontinued. Cue tears.

The Sweet Release

- The universal truth: there's no joy like unhooking your bra the moment you walk through the door.
- Bonus points if you manage to Houdini it off through your sleeve. A true superpower.

Sports Bra Struggles

- Putting it on feels like a wrestling match; taking it off is an escape room challenge.
- You burn more calories getting it off than during your workout.

Hair Today, Gone Tomorrow

The War on Body Hair

- The eternal debate: wax, shave, or embrace the fuzz? Whatever you choose, regrowth is always itching to torment you.
- You shave your legs, and it's like a rain dance—cue jumper weather the next day.

Bad Hair Days

- The days when your hair flat-out refuses to cooperate, no matter how many serums, sprays, or whispered prayers you use.

Granny's Gripes

- Ponytails become your best mate. Add a headband, and suddenly, it's a *look*.

Wardrobe Woes

1. Pocketless Pants

Why do men's jeans get deep, practical pockets, while women's pants get decorative, useless ones? Where are we supposed to stash our snacks?

Whoever invented fake pockets clearly never had to carry keys, a phone, or lip balm.

The High Heels Dilemma

They make you look fabulous... but at what cost? Blisters, aching feet, and the sensation of walking on knives by the end of the night. You bring flats "just in case", but still end up barefoot halfway through the event.

The Dressing Room Mirror Conspiracy

Why do clothes look amazing in-store and tragic at home? Are they using enchanted mirrors?

You realise the dress has an invisible zipper that requires a full team to fasten.

Monthly Mysteries

The Purse Stash Panic

That sinking feeling when you dig through your bag and can't find a tampon or pad. You're MacGyvering a solution in a public loo. A stranger offers you one. Sisterhood restored.

PMS Perils

One minute you're sobbing over a dog food ad, the next you're furious because the toaster took too long. Cravings so specific, only peanut butter pretzels dipped in chocolate will do.

The Unpredictable Arrival

It's early, it's late, it's *exactly* when you're wearing white. Mother Nature loves a dramatic entrance.

Makeup Misadventures

The Eyeliner Wing Battle

It starts with the goal of "just a little flick," and 15 minutes later, you've got Cleopatra wings.

Repeat on the other eye until they match (*spoiler: they never match*).

The Foundation Fiasco

You think you've nailed your shade, but in natural light, you realise you're an Oompa Loompa.

Yet somehow, influencers still look flawless in the same shade.

Mascara Mishaps

You sneeze right after applying it, and suddenly, you're in full raccoon mode.

The Unseen Emotional Load

The Mental Checklist

Remembering birthdays, booking doctor's appointments, tracking school events... the list is never-ending.

You're basically the family's unpaid PA.

Smile More Syndrome

The infuriating moment when a stranger tells you to smile—because your neutral face isn't for *their* benefit.

Juggling It All

Career, relationships, family, friendships—you're multitasking at Olympic level.

You might feel like you're barely holding it together, but to everyone else, you're Wonder Woman.

Granny's Gripes

This chapter captures the humour, absurdity, and shared struggles of womanhood. After all, the trials may be many—but so is the camaraderie that gets us through them all.

Chapter 11:
Decluttering – Keeping the Memories, Ditching the Stuff

There are two sides to this story.

The first is emotional.

The second is utterly exasperating.

The Emotional Side: Sorting Through a Life Well-Lived

I first encountered the ache of decluttering when my mum decided to downsize.

✓ She was practical.

✓ She was sensible.

✓ She was also completely unbothered.

She handed us boxes and asked, "Do you want any of this before I get rid of it?"

This is a reasonable thing to do. But it felt so wrong. Like we were acknowledging that her life was wrapping up sooner rather than later.

And when the time came for her to move into a nursing home, she gave us permission to clear out her house and sell it.

Her *home*. Not just a building—a place where:

✓ She cooked meals.

✓ She talked to us on the phone.

✓ She organised her bingo nights and volunteer work.

✓ She slept, dreamed, and lived.

Then, one January morning, on a bright, sunny day, she left us. And we had to do it all over again.

Granny's Gripes

This time, her *room*.

✓ Her clothes.

✓ Her photos.

✓ Her furniture.

✓ Her toothbrush, pyjamas, and dressing gown.

The bathroom was the worst. So ordinary, yet so personal.

And then, of course, there were her teeth.

Yes. Her dentures.

At this point, my brother and I were so overwhelmed that the only logical question to ask was: *"Do we keep them or donate them?"*

That moment of absurdity saved us. Because when you're drowning in grief, sometimes you just need to laugh.

But the truth is, decluttering someone else's life is brutal.

Because it's not just 'stuff.' It's proof that they were here.

The Next Round: My Own Decluttering Battle

Years later, it was my turn.

When I retired and moved interstate, I had to face my own mountain of "treasures."

✓ I was leaving a beautiful country cottage and moving into a unit in the suburbs.

✓ It was time to decide what stayed and what went.

✓ I was ready… or so I thought.

Naturally, I assumed the family would want some of these things. After all, I'd kept them safe for decades.

The Brutal Reality: They Don't Want It.

So, I asked the grandkids.

Christine Smith

Would anyone like…

✓ Handmade knee blankets?

✓ Handcrafted cushion covers?

✓ My teak sewing cabinet from Singapore, bought by my mum in 1968?

✓ One grandchild took the sewing cabinet. *One.*

✓ The knee blankets? No thanks.

✓ The cushion covers? Absolutely not.

And the best part? The responses.

💬 One grandchild, ever so tactful:

"Oh, thank you, but I don't think I could do them justice."

💬 The other, brutally honest:

"No thanks, not my thing."

And that, my friends, is when I realised something very important.

Lesson Learned: No One Cares About Your Stuff But You.

The things I thought were treasures? Just clutter to someone else.

✓ Handmade quilts? Outdated.

✓ Crystal bowls? No one wants to polish them.

✓ Silverware? Too hard to clean.

✓ Ornate furniture? Not "modern" enough.

Meanwhile, I had been carefully preserving these items like a museum curator… for an audience that did not exist.

My New Approach: Use It or Lose It

After that harsh wake-up call, I changed my thinking.

✓ No more "saving for best."

Granny's Gripes

✓ No more hoarding things that "might be useful one day."

✓ If I don't use it, it gets sold or donated.

Because I refuse to let my son spend a month going through my stuff, wondering why I owned 12 cake plates but only ever made three cakes.

The Emotional Side: What Do We Actually Keep?

Not everything can go. Some things stay—not because they're valuable, but because they matter.

✓ My parents' canteen of cutlery and dinner service. I use them every day.

✓ My grandmother's kitchen utensils. I still use them.

✓ My aunt's 100-year-old dessert bowl. It has history.

✓ Anything that reminds me of people, not just things.

And that's the balance, isn't it?

Keeping the memories, not the clutter.

Final Thought: How Are Other People Handling This?

I know I'm not the only one in this decluttering dilemma.

✓ Have you started sorting through your things so your kids won't have to later?

✓ Did they want anything, or are they planning to torch it all and start fresh?

✓ What's the one thing you can't bear to part with?

Because if there's one universal truth, it's this:

We all leave behind stuff.

The real question is… will anyone want it?

Chapter 12:
Can You Not Plan Your Own Trip?

(Or: If You Need This Much Help, Maybe Just Stay Home.)

There was a time, back in the glorious age of competence, when people either booked through a travel agent or did their own damn research.

✓ You collected brochures.

✓ You read newspaper travel columns.

✓ You had to put in effort.

Then came the internet, putting unlimited information at our fingertips. These days, I book everything myself with the precision of a brain surgeon, because one wrong click can cost you thousands.

I learned this lesson the easy way (by researching). An acquaintance of mine? She learned it the expensive way, by accidentally cancelling all her flights instead of editing them.

✓ She lost every cent she'd saved for her once-in-a-lifetime trip.

✓ The airline showed zero mercy.

✓ And she hadn't bought travel insurance, she was "waiting until just before the trip."

A masterclass in how not to travel.

The Epidemic of Decision Paralysis

Somewhere along the way, people forgot how to make decisions.

✓ They can't pick an airline.

✓ They can't set a budget.

✓ They don't know where to stay.

✓ They need a Facebook poll to decide if they should pack a raincoat.

Granny's Gripes

How do these people function in daily life? If you need strangers to plan every part of your trip, maybe international travel isn't for you.

The Most Ridiculous Travel Questions I've Seen

I'm in a few travel groups, and trust me, the questions range from mildly lazy to downright alarming.

✓ "What's the best airline?"

Do you want luxury, the cheapest fare, or just to land alive? Be specific.

✓ "How much should I budget?"

Are you backpacking or living like Italian royalty? I don't know your life.

✓ "What's the best phone lanyard?"

I'm sorry, but if that overwhelms you, should you even be leaving the country?

At this rate, people will soon be asking:

? "What's the best way to use a toilet in Italy?"

? "Should I walk forward or backward through Rome?"

? "How do I breathe in Venice?"

For the love of espresso, just Google it.

My 'Just Showing Off' Theory

Some of these questions are so basic, I refuse to believe people are really that clueless.

Which leaves only one explanation: they just want us all to know they're going to Italy.

✓ "What's the best way to spend six weeks in Tuscany?"

(Translation: Look at me, I can afford six weeks in Tuscany!)

✓ "Should I stay at a private villa in Amalfi or a boutique hotel in Positano?"

(Translation: Please be jealous of my struggle.)

✓ "Can someone help me plan my dream trip to Italy?"

(Translation: Shower me with validation and tell me how lucky I am.)

If you're just posting for bragging rights, at least be honest about it.

The People Who Can't Be Bothered to Google

Newsflash: Google exists.

✓ Want to know what to see in Rome? Google.

✓ Want to compare airlines? Google.

✓ Need to set a budget? Google.

✓ Want to know the best phone lanyard? Who cares, Google it anyway.

If your first instinct is to ask strangers to do all the work for you, I have serious concerns about how you function in the real world.

The Harsh Truth: If You Can't Plan a Trip, Maybe Stay Home

Look, travel isn't that hard.

✓ If you can book a doctor's appointment, you can book a flight.

✓ If you can buy groceries, you can set a travel budget.

✓ If you can choose a restaurant, you can pick a hotel.

If you genuinely can't handle these basic tasks on your own?

Maybe international travel isn't for you.

Final Thought: Some People Shouldn't Be Allowed Out of the Country

Yes, planning a trip takes effort.

Granny's Gripes

But if you need Facebook to hold your hand through every single decision, how are you going to survive in an actual foreign country?

✓ If you get lost, you'll need to figure it out.

✓ If something goes wrong, you'll have to deal with it.

✓ If you can't decide what to pack without a poll, you're in trouble.

So if you truly can't make a single decision on your own?

Stay home. Just... stay home.

Chapter 13:
The Male Contribution to Society – Manspreading on Planes

Ah, the Joys of Modern Air Travel

A delightful experience: crammed into a tin can at 30,000 feet, given one measly ice cube in your drink, and expected to maintain some semblance of sanity while wedged between strangers.

Still, I'd been smart this time. I booked a window seat.

A tactical move: one side protected, one side to defend. Perfect.

Or so I thought.

The Manspreader Arrives

Enter the man to my right.

✓ He wasn't large in body, just in personal space ambition.

✓ His legs sprawled wide, as if preparing for a deadlift.

✓ His elbows jutted out, claiming the armrest like a colonial explorer discovering "new land".

I eyed him. He was oblivious.

I shifted. He didn't adjust.

I sighed. He remained in his imperial stance.

I couldn't help but wonder:

Are their balls truly that enormous?

Is this a medical condition I should feel sympathy for?

Or was it just territorial male nonsense, a subconscious belief that any space left unoccupied must be conquered?

I leaned back in my seat, already mentally preparing for battle.

The Passive-Aggressive Warning Shot

Granny's Gripes

First up: the patented loud cough. Not just any cough, the kind that makes cats bolt and toddlers freeze.

It had worked on rude shop assistants, queue hoverers, and once, on a particularly inconsiderate yoga instructor who wouldn't stop talking about her juice cleanse.

The result this time? Nothing. Not even a flinch.

He was deep into an in-flight action movie, noise-cancelling headphones insulating him from my growing rage.

Time for Direct Action

I turned, smiling sweetly, the kind of smile that often precedes a polite, devastating scolding.

"Excuse me, young man," I cooed, voice steeped in faux elderly wisdom.

"Would you mind keeping your legs in your own personal bubble? Some of us enjoy breathing room."

Startled, he blinked.

He removed one headphone, just one, a power move I did not appreciate.

"Huh?"

I pointed. "Your legs. They're currently violating international airspace."

He hesitated. He looked down, as if seeing them for the first time.

After a disgruntled mutter, likely about feminists or personal freedoms, he finally, reluctantly, moved his legs closer together.

Victory.

But Why Is Manspreading a Thing?

As the plane levelled off into smooth cruising, I sipped my one sip of white wine (because that's all they pour into those thimble-sized plastic cups) and pondered the ongoing phenomenon.

✓ Is it biological? A deep-seated evolutionary instinct?

✓ Cultural? A misguided belief that men require the spatial equivalent of a small planet to sit comfortably?

✓ Or is it just plain stubbornness? A refusal to acknowledge that airplane seats are not, in fact, thrones?

Maybe there's a study on this somewhere.

Maybe universities should pause their research on cow farts and focus on why some men believe their knees must always be four feet apart.

Final Thought: The Next Chapter

I glanced at my tiny tray table, barely large enough to hold a drink and my sanity, and smirked.

This would make a fantastic chapter in my book.

"Granny Gripes: The Modern Plight" will have an entire section dedicated to manspreading: on planes, on trains, in waiting rooms.

Because if men want all that extra space, they can have it.

Just not at the expense of my personal comfort.

Chapter 14:
DIY Disasters & Home Projects Gone Wrong

(Or: "I Came, I Saw, I Swore.")

There Are Two Kinds of People in This World:

✓ Those who walk into Bunnings with a shopping list and stick to it.

✓ And me, who walks in for some screws and leaves with a trolley full of potential chaos.

Because, my friends, I love Bunnings.

The smell of fresh-cut wood.

The aisles filled with endless possibilities.

The pure joy of the sausage sizzle.

And let's not forget Aisle 15, the party aisle, and Aisle 29, where dreams (and sausages) come true.

Oh, and did you know? You can hire a stripper for $34…

I'll let you sit with that thought for a moment.

(Alright, it's a wallpaper stripper. But for that price, I was briefly intrigued.)

DIY Ambitions, Bunnings Delusions

With great confidence and a sausage in one hand, I set out to transform my home like some sort of retired renovation queen.

Armed with all the right tools (or at least the ones that looked important), I wheeled my overloaded trolley to the car and thought, this will be easy.

Hindsight is a wonderful thing.

IKEA Rage – Step 1: Open the Box. Step 2: Cry.

Christine Smith

Next stop: IKEA.

I know, I know, it's a dangerous game. But sometimes, a woman needs a bookshelf.

Back home, I opened the flat-pack box and immediately regretted every life choice I'd ever made.

✓ A hundred tiny screws.

✓ An Allen key the size of a toothpick.

✓ Instructions featuring a cheerful cartoon man who has clearly never built this nonsense himself.

I tried to follow the "simple steps", but IKEA manuals are written in riddles.

✓ Is that piece meant to be upside down?

✓ Why are there leftover screws?

✓ What's the Swedish word for help?!

Three hours later, the bookshelf was standing.

Barely.

It leaned at an angle that defied every known law of physics,

not quite a bookshelf, not quite modern art.

Honestly, I considered submitting it to an exhibition.

The Neighbourhood Summoning Ritual

At this point, I had two options: admit defeat… or cheat.

Enter: the hammer.

Why? Because Gaz, my neighbour over the back fence, has a sixth sense for DIY disasters.

✓ The moment he hears a hammer and a few colourful words, my phone dings.

Granny's Gripes

✓ "What are you doing? Can I help?"

✓ The system works.

Minutes later, Gaz appears, amused, but prepared.

✓ "You do know that shelf is meant to be straight, right?"

✓ "Are these extra screws… important, I ask?"

✓ "What the hell have you done?"

Oh, how we laughed.

(Well, he laughed. I drank tea and questioned my existence.)

Pinterest vs Reality – A Cautionary Tale

You'd think I'd have learnt my lesson. But no, I had one more DIY dream to destroy.

Scrolling through Pinterest one night, I stumbled upon a "simple" home hack: turning an old ladder into a plant shelf.

✓ It looked stunning.

✓ It looked effortless.

✓ It lied to me.

When Plants Attack

Out came the ladder from the shed, slightly rickety but full of potential.

✓ I carefully placed my potted plants on each step.

✓ I admired my handiwork.

✓ I stepped back to bask in the glow of achievement.

And then, in slow motion, the entire thing collapsed.

✓ Soil everywhere.

✓ Plants rolling across the floor like escapees.

✓ Milo, my cat, staring at me with unfiltered judgment.

Christine Smith

My home no longer looked like an elegant Pinterest dream.

It looked like a crime scene from Gardening Gone Wrong.

Final Thought: DIY Is a Humbling Experience

They say DIY builds character.

I say it builds rage.

But in the end, it's not about perfection.

It's about:

✓ The laughter.

✓ The Bunnings sausage sizzle.

✓ The satisfaction of finishing a project, no matter how much help you needed.

So if you ever hear a hammer and some mild cursing, just know…

I'm at it again.

Chapter 15: Doctor's Appointments & Medical Mayhem

The Waiting Room Twilight Zone

Arriving on time. Wondering if time forgot you.

The Google Diagnosis Spiral

Searched for "mild headache." Now convinced you're dying.

I sat in the waiting room, clutching my appointment card like it was a boarding pass to somewhere I'd really rather not go.

The chairs were the usual kind,

✓ too low

✓ too firm

✓ suspiciously sticky

And the clock ticked loud enough to ensure we all knew we were, in fact, wasting our precious minutes on Earth.

This is the point where most people sigh dramatically.

Not me.

I people-watch.

The cast of characters was classic:

✓ A man with a cough that could rattle windows.

✓ Two toddlers tearing around like caffeinated whippets.

✓ A woman reading a book upside down, and somehow winning at it.

Across from me, a snorer was in full voice, mouth wide open, dreaming of better places, probably anywhere but here.

But today, I was feeling… cautiously optimistic.

Christine Smith

Because my new doctor, a no-nonsense Greek marvel, had so far been on time for my appointments. A miracle. Each time I entered his consulting room; I wondered which slice of blunt wisdom he would meter out this time. Last appointment, he barely looked up before prescribing:

"Lose weight. Wear proper shoes."

(Translation: Stop faffing about and put the ballet flats away, lady.)

It was a refreshing change from my lovely Melbourne doctor, Shelley.

Shelley was kind beyond words, but often caught mid-rescue, gently talking suicidal patients down from emotional cliffs while the rest of us waited, checking our watches and adjusting to the reality that our 10:15 appointment might happen closer to noon.

Not that I could wait long. My car was parked on a meter. And Melbourne's meter-police? Ruthless.

After feeding the beast twice and nervously eyeing every fluorescent-vested figure that passed, I gave up, rebooked, and fled before getting fined.

Medical mayhem indeed.

"Waiting rooms: where time stretches, patience shrinks, and laughter is the only prescription that doesn't require a refill."

Back to today.

I checked the time. Five minutes past my appointment. A record!

I leaned back, carefully (sticky chair, remember?), and smiled.

Even here, in the waiting room twilight zone, there was always a story.

Beside me, a woman muttered "bloody WebMD" while scrolling on her phone.

I felt for her. One innocent Google search for "mild headache" and next thing you're planning your will.

A toddler screamed like he was auditioning for an opera.

Granny's Gripes

His brother upended an entire box of tissues onto the floor.

Their mother, in saintly silence, handed the receptionist a crumpled Medicare card with one hand while fishing a Lego piece out of a stranger's handbag with the other.

We are warriors, we women.

Eventually, my name was called.

I stood, tucked my book under my arm, and walked into the consulting room, steeling myself for the reality check to come.

Perhaps a stern word about posture.

Or shoe orthotics.

Maybe a quick lecture on iron intake, delivered with the soothing tenderness of a brick to the forehead.

One thing was certain:

✓ It would be blunt.

✓ It would be correct.

✓ It would be over quickly.

A bit like life itself, if you think about it.

And honestly?

After years of chaos, Melbourne meters, toddlers, coughers, and sticky chairs, I've decided…

I rather like it this way.

Straight to the point. Proper shoes and all.

Chapter 16:
Parenting: If You Won't Do It, Who Will?

I know this is a prickly topic, but honestly, I'm losing patience.

Every day on the news here in Australia, it's another carjacking. Another home invasion. Another shopkeeper terrorised.

By kids.

Under fifteen.

How on earth did we get here?

Growing up with a Quartermaster for a father and a mother who didn't tolerate backchat, we learned a few basic rules early:

✓ Do as you're told.

✓ Be where you said you'd be.

✓ Face the consequences if you weren't.

Not that we were saints.

We bent the rules. We got into trouble. But it was smart trouble, the kind that might earn you a clip around the ear at home, not a visit to the police station.

And if you really mucked up?

There was always the shadowy threat of Borstal, a brutal-sounding place where no one wanted to end up.

(I was clever enough not to get caught, and cheeky enough to know my limits.)

And the police?

We respected them.

Or at the very least, we respected the fact that if they caught you, you were done for. No lectures. No "processing your emotions." Just consequences.

Granny's Gripes

Imagine that.

Schools Are Not Substitute Parents

I've got no problem with schools teaching real-life skills:

✓ Cooking? Yes, please.

✓ Budgeting? Absolutely.

✓ First aid? Essential.

✓ Changing a tyre? Honestly, more useful than algebra ever was.

But now I see parents expecting schools to teach:

✓ Discipline.

✓ Respect for authority.

✓ Emotional regulation.

✓ Basic human decency.

That's not education.

That's parenting.

When did raising your own children become someone else's job?

The "I Can't Control Them" Lie

Every time I hear a parent say, "I can't control my kid," I want to ask:

✓ Who pays the bills?

✓ Who puts food on the table?

✓ Who sets the rules in your house?

Kids will push boundaries, it's practically their job.

But ours?

Ours is to hold the line.

And if you don't?

✓ Eventually, the police will.

✓ And trust me, they won't give a toss about your gentle parenting philosophy.

The Parents Expecting Society to Clean Up Their Mess

Every day, it's the same chorus:

✓ "The government should do more."

✓ "Schools should intervene."

✓ "The system failed my kid."

Meanwhile, their twelve-year-old is out at 2 a.m., robbing a servo with a kitchen knife, and apparently no one saw it coming?

Really?

It's simple:

✓ Be the parent.

✓ Set the rules. Enforce them.

✓ And if they won't listen? Find a way to make them.

Or else?

✓ Society will do it for you, and you will not like the results.

Some People Shouldn't Have Had Kids (There, I Said It)

Unpopular opinion? Maybe.

True? Absolutely.

✓ If you're not willing to discipline your kids, don't have them.

✓ If you're too lazy to teach them how to act like civilised humans, don't have them.

✓ If you think the world owes you childcare for life, don't have them.

Children are not accessories.

Granny's Gripes

They're not little emotional support trophies.

They're a responsibility, and a damn big one at that.

The Bottom Line: Take Responsibility or Shut Up

When I was growing up, we called it benign neglect.

We were left to entertain ourselves, roam the backyard, invent games, but all within clear, enforced boundaries.

We felt loved. We felt safe.

And we knew exactly where the lines were drawn.

Today's kids aren't bored because they have nothing to do.

They're bored because no one's taught them how to be.

✓ Grow a veggie patch.

✓ Join Scouts or Girls' Brigade.

✓ Get outside and climb a tree.

And if we ever dared say we were bored?

My mother had a fix:

✓ A mop.

✓ A broom.

✓ And a chore list the length of your arm.

Funny how quickly we learned to entertain ourselves.

Bottom line?

You had kids.

Now act like it.

Because if you don't step up,

✓ The police will.

✓ The courts will.

✓ And society at large will.

And believe me, it'll be a lot less forgiving than a stern telling-off at home.

"Boundaries aren't cruelty , they're love with a backbone."

Chapter 17:
Support Farmers – "If You Eat Food, You Should Care About Farmers"

(Or: "Supermarkets: Handy for Cat Food, Hopeless for Freshness.")

Look, I'm no saint.

Yes, I shop at the supermarket, mostly for essential life supplies like cat biscuits (Milo insists) and emergency chocolate (who doesn't?).

But when it comes to real food, fruit, veg, the stuff you actually want to taste, I head to my local greengrocer.

(I know that's a privilege, and not everyone has the option.)

Not only do I save money, but I know the farmers are getting a better deal.

And when that produce is grown just down the road?

You can taste the difference.

A real tomato smells like a tomato, just like my uncle's did in Doncaster, or like my friend's still do in her Portsmouth allotment. Not like a vaguely sad water balloon.

Here in Australia, I'm lucky to live near orchards, farm shops, and proper farmers' markets.

(And yes, I attempt to grow a few herbs in the backyard too, some more successfully than others.)

Small businesses like 100 Miles at Adelaide Airport (local food within, you guessed it, 100 miles) and Can Cook | Well Fed in the UK are showing the way:

Buy direct. Eat seasonal. Support farmers.

It's not rocket science. It's just common sense. (Remember that?)

Why Supermarkets Aren't Really Your Friend

Christine Smith

Supermarkets love to talk about 'supporting local farmers.'

Meanwhile, back at the ranch:

- ✔ They pay farmers peanuts.
- ✔ They import apples from overseas while local ones rot in crates.
- ✔ They reject perfectly good produce because it doesn't look like a runway model.

And as for governments?

- ✔ Family farms are vanishing, thanks to sky-high inheritance taxes.
- ✔ Prime farmland is being sold off, for solar farms and shopping centres.

(Here's a wild idea: stick the solar panels on top of the supermarkets. No? Too logical?)

Farmers' Markets: The Comeback We Need

The good news?

People are waking up.

(We usually get there. Eventually. After three coffees.)

- ✔ Farm shops are booming in the UK.
- ✔ Farmers' markets are buzzing here in Australia.
- ✔ Some towns are even setting up co-ops to buy directly from farmers.

Imagine it:

- ✔ Fresh, affordable food.
- ✔ Local farmers getting paid fairly.
- ✔ Communities that actually know each other again.

Supermarkets only win if we keep handing them our money.

Time to get a bit stubborn about it, don't you think?

Granny's Gripes

Kids Think Food Comes from a Packet (Spoiler: It Doesn't)

Today's kids can name fifty TikTok stars without blinking...

But ask where milk comes from? They'll point at the fridge.

We've got to do better.

Kids should know:

- ✔ Wheat becomes bread, not "comes from a packet."
- ✔ Milk comes from cows, not cartons.
- ✔ Strawberries grow in dirt, not in shiny plastic tubs.

Imagine a generation that could grow a tomato instead of just photographing one for Instagram.

(There's a thought.)

It's Simple: Support Real Food, or Lose It

If we want real food, real farmers, and real flavour, here's the game plan:

- ✔ Buy local whenever you can.
- ✔ Visit farmers' markets and farm shops.
- ✔ Ask where your food actually comes from.
- ✔ Teach the next generation how to plant a seed, and watch it grow.

Because if we don't?

The future menu starts to look a lot like fake meat, processed sludge, and lettuce that's travelled further than your last holiday.

And honestly? We deserve better than that.

"Good farmers grow good food. Support them like your life (and your dinner plate) depends on it... because it does."

5 Easy Ways to Support Farmers

Christine Smith

- Shop at farmers' markets or farm shops
- Buy seasonal produce
- Ask questions about where your food comes from
- Grow something, even a pot of herbs
- Teach kids that food doesn't grow in supermarkets

"Support the people who grow your food, because Uber Eats can't deliver a harvest."

Chapter 18: Charity Op Shops – The Corporate Cash Grab Disguised as Altruism

(Or: "How Did a Bag of Donated Clothes Become a Luxury Purchase?")

Once Upon a Time, Charity Shops Were for Charity

You could walk into an op shop, rifle through the racks, and come out with quality clothes at prices that didn't make you weep. It was a place for low-income families, students, and the occasional thrifty shopper hunting a bargain.

But that was then.

These days? Forget it. Charity shops have morphed into corporate retail chains with a moral superiority complex. The big ones, the religious ones, the shops run on the backs of volunteers and Work for the Dole job seekers, are no longer in the business of helping. Oh no.

They're in the business of making money.

"It's for charity!"

(Translation: We'll charge you more than Kmart for the same shirt.)

Here's the scam:

✓ They get all their stock for free, every single item donated by well-meaning people trying to do good.

✓ They sell those same items at prices that would make a boutique blush. I once saw a Target-brand blouse in a charity shop for $15. It was probably $12 new.

✓ They refuse to admit they're a business. But make no mistake, they are. And unlike actual businesses, they:

Don't pay tax.

Get government subsidies.

Still pay their managers bonuses.

Bonuses?! For what? Standing at the register, sighing at customers who dare to ask why a second-hand teapot costs $30?

And don't even think about donating anything that isn't "on-trend."

✓ Not a big brand? Rejected.

✓ Too 'outdated'? Straight to landfill.

✓ Could be given to someone in need? No chance, unless they can pay for it.

"People Are Donating Less!" Gee, I Wonder Why…

Maybe donations are drying up because people are sick of being ripped off.

Once, people donated because they trusted their old clothes and goods would be sold cheaply or given to those who needed them. Now?

✓ They sell their stuff online instead. Sites like Vinted, eBay, and Facebook Marketplace let them pocket the cash themselves, why donate to a "charity" that's just another greedy middleman?

✓ They take items to small, independent op shops, the ones run by church groups in community halls, not those slick retail setups.

✓ They swap clothes instead. Ever heard of swap-and-save stores? Bring in what you don't want, trade for store credit. Simple. Practical. Fair.

And charity shops dare complain people aren't donating as much? Cry me a river. Maybe if they stopped acting like department stores, people would trust them again.

The Glorious Rise of Small, Independent Op Shops

Not all op shops are created equal.

While the corporate charity giants try to convince us a pre-loved pair of jeans is worth $40, the little guys are still doing it right.

Granny's Gripes

✓ The tiny church-run shop opposite Coles in Unley? A hidden gem. Volunteers who actually care, prices that reflect what op shops should be about, and an atmosphere where you don't feel scammed.

✓ The community swap shop in Victor Harbor where my daughter got entire bags of clothes for $20, a lifesaver when he needed endless changes due to my grandson's leukemia treatment.

✓ Independent thrift stores in Melbourne where trendy tops cost next to nothing, because fashion shouldn't be a luxury.

These places remember what charity shops used to be about: helping people, not profiting off them.

Then there are the 'hire a rack' shops, popular especially in Adelaide. Some specialise in high-end designer clothes, others everyday wear. They encourage you to clean out your closet, hire a rack, and make some money yourself.

How Did We Let This Happen?

Once upon a time, charity shops were:

✓ Affordable.

✓ Accessible.

✓ Vital resources for low-income families.

Now? In my opinion, they're just retail scams milking government subsidies while managers pocket bonuses off free labour.

And the worst part?

✓ They push the "eco-friendly" and "ethical" narrative to justify price hikes.

✓ They guilt-trip people into paying more, pretending it's all about "helping the community."

✓ They dump tons of unsold stock into landfill, because heaven forbid they lower prices or give things away to people who actually need them.

Christine Smith

Final Thought: What Can We Do?

If charity shops want to behave like profit-driven businesses, maybe it's time we treat them like one, and take our money elsewhere.

✓ Support small, independent op shops.

✓ Use online platforms to sell or swap.

✓ Call out charity store price-gouging (there are many on TikTok doing exactly that).

✓ If you want to donate, choose places that give items away, not just sell them at boutique prices.

Because at the end of the day:

If you charge boutique prices for second-hand clothes, you're not a charity.

You're just another greedy shop in disguise.

Chapter 19.
Everyday irritations that should be illegal

You might need another cup for this chapter, it's long!

Fifteen (15) Household Annoyances That Will One Day Push Me Over the Edge

1. The English Language Is Gaslighting Us

"You think you understand the rules, then BOOM, some ridiculous new exception ruins everything."

- Tough, though, thought, through.
- Read (present) vs. Read (past).
- Dessert vs. Desert.

If English were a person, they'd be banned from writing instruction manuals.

What's the Solution? (Besides Crying?)

Honestly, at this point, we should either:

A) Simplify spelling so it actually makes sense.

B) Give up and let autocorrect decide.

C) Just start making up new words like Shakespeare did.

I vote C.

Let's ditch the silent letters, make everything phonetic, and see what happens.

(Spoiler: Chaos. But fun chaos.)

Spelling Rules That Should Be Outlawed

a. Why Does 'C' Exist?

If 'C' makes a 'K' sound (cat, car) or an 'S' sound (ceiling, circle), WHY do we need it?

Replace it with 'K' or 'S' and move on:

- ✓ 'Kool' instead of 'Cool.'
- ✓ 'Sirkus' instead of 'Circus.'

b. Why Does 'PH' Make an 'F' Sound?

- Phone → Fone
- Elephant → Elefant
- Pharmacy → Why isn't it just FARMACY?!

English is like that one friend who takes the long way just to be difficult.

c. The Ough Nightmare

English decided 'ough' can have 9 different pronunciations, including:

- ✓ Through → 'throo'
- ✓ Though → 'tho'
- ✓ Tough → 'tuff'
- ✓ Thought → 'thawt'
- ✓ Bough → 'bow' (like take a bow)
- ✓ Cough → 'coff'

I give up. Who invented this chaos? They need to be held accountable.

...And from Twitter:

- Stephen Killick – add **plough** to the 'ough' section
- foodbysimmy – T in Pinot...I guess it's trouble if we haven't any

d. The 'Colonel' Incident

There is no 'R' in 'colonel,' yet we pronounce it 'kernel.'

Excuse me, WHAT?

Granny's Gripes

Meanwhile, 'kernel' already exists as a separate word.

If I were learning English as a second language, I would simply walk away.

The Bizarrely Spelled Words That Mock Us Daily

- ✓ **Wednesday** → That 'D' is silent and pointless. Let's just call it Wensday and move on.
- ✓ **Receipt** → WHY IS THERE A 'P'?! Who allowed this? 'Reciet' is fine.
- ✓ **Sword** → The 'W' is doing NOTHING. 'Sord' is enough.
- ✓ **Giraffe** → Why 'FF'? Just spell it 'Jiraff' and be done.
- ✓ **Lasagna** → This is spaghetti's weird cousin and does NOT need a silent 'G.'

The Final Proposal: Let's Fix English.

Ban silent letters and simplify spelling:

- ✓ Knock → Nok
- ✓ Gnome → Nome
- ✓ Science → Syence
- ✓ Queue → Q

There. Fixed it.

Phrases That Bug Me:

- **Calm down**, especially on social media.
- **How can I help you, luv?**
- **Next...** (when waiting in line)

Phrases That Fry My Twitter Friends' Brains:

- Jenny Mortimer – "calm down", a phrase guaranteed to do the opposite.

- Jenny Mortimer – "just relax"
- YellowFin Tune – "here's why"
- Stephen Killick – "reaching out", I am just sending you a bloody email.
- Stephen Killick – "going forward", It's hard to do backwards with time.
- Stephen Killick – quantifying "unique", almost always redundant.
- Stu Jordan – "circling back"
- Glen Edwards – "lush"
- TiminBrum – "obviously"
- Arch Stanton – "woke"
- Simon Forrester – "doing whatever it takes" and "going forward"

2. The Internet Provider Monopoly: A Scam, Plain and Simple

Oh, you'd like an alternative provider?

TOO BAD.

Every phone line here belongs to one company.

- ✓ Bad service?
- ✓ Outrageous prices?
- ✓ No other options?

Classic monopoly behavior.

When you call customer service to complain:

- ✓ They "test your connection" (which magically works fine while they're on the line).
- ✓ They blame "network congestion."

Granny's Gripes

- ✓ They suggest resetting your router, as if we haven't tried that 57 times already.

The Unforgivable Dead Zones

Inside the house? Nothing.

Outside? Full 5G, like I've stepped into the future.

So now I'm forced to take important phone calls pacing the street like a madwoman, waving my phone around as if summoning the gods.

Do I know what the neighbors think? No.

Do I care? Not much.

Will I one day take a call in my nightie just to make a point? Possibly.

Frankly, if that leads to being arrested by a nice man in uniform, maybe I won't complain.

Honestly, how is this still happening in 2025?

The Final Solution: Moving into the Street?

Since the only place I get full 5G is outside, my choices are:

1. Continue marching up and down the street like an escaped lunatic.
2. Set up a small folding chair and take business calls on the sidewalk.
3. Go outside in my nightie and see if I get arrested.

Honestly, I'm considering option three.

If I can't have fast internet, at least I can have a good story.

What do you think, should I fight for better Wi-Fi, or embrace my new role as "That Crazy Woman on the Sidewalk"?

3. The Slow Internet Rage Spiral (Modern Technology, My Ass)

- ✓ Wi-Fi working perfectly, until you need it.
- ✓ Buffering in 2025?! How is this still a thing?

- ✓ "Your download will be ready in 5 minutes", Lies. It'll take 3 hours.
- ✓ The smart TV remote requiring 57 button presses just to open Netflix.

We have AI, self-driving cars, and fridges that order milk.

But consistent Wi-Fi? Apparently that's too much to ask.

Yet here I am, living in the Adelaide foothills, buffering a YouTube video like it's 2006.

(Solution: Throw it all in the sea. Except you need Wi-Fi to complain about it online.)

4. Keyboard Warriors: The Armchair Experts Nobody Asked For

Ah yes, the keyboard warrior, that magnificent creature who emerges from the murky depths of the internet only to criticise, belittle, and generally suck the joy out of life. Today, my entry for a cooking competition (one I've been involved in for years, might I add) attracted a couple of these delightful specimens who seemingly exist solely to diminish other people's achievements.

And why? Because they can.

These armchair reviewers wouldn't dare utter a peep in person, but give them a screen, Wi-Fi, and a misplaced sense of superiority, and suddenly they're world-class critics on everything they've never done themselves.

✓ Never cooked professionally? Doesn't stop them tearing down an award-winning dish.

✓ Never written a book? They'll gladly tell you why yours is rubbish.

✓ Never achieved anything remotely remarkable? Ah, but they have opinions, and by God, you WILL hear them.

Now, I could have ignored them, but where's the fun in that? Instead, they got a generous serving of sarcasm, because really, if they're going to waste their time being miserable, I might as well make it entertaining.

But here's the best bit: while they're gleefully throwing shade, they're simultaneously branding themselves as bitter, insecure, and completely unhinged.

The truth? I feel sorry for them. Anyone who spends their days trying to tear down people who are doing something with their lives must be profoundly unfulfilled. I'm out here cooking, writing, and enjoying life. They're just lurking in the comments, waiting to pounce.

So, to all the keyboard warriors out there: maybe go outside? Touch some grass? Accomplish literally anything? And if that's too much effort, at least find a hobby that doesn't involve being insufferable online.

5. The Teabag Packet Wrapper Battle (Why Is Making Tea a Struggle?)

✓ The outer plastic wrap that won't peel.

✓ The inner foil that refuses to tear.

✓ The teabag string that always falls into the cup.

✓ The missing 'D' in refrigerator but not fridge.

(Solution: Go back to loose-leaf tea and start drinking gin instead.)

6. The Toothpaste Stopper Fiasco (Why Is It So Hard to Brush My Teeth?)

✓ The 'twist-off' cap that doesn't actually pierce the foil.

✓ The tiny silver seal that sticks to your fingers.

✓ The over-squeeze disaster that sends toothpaste flying into the sink.

✓ The existential crisis of trying to open new packaging before coffee.

(Solution: Scissors. Always scissors.)

7. The Customer Service Black Hole (Press 1 to Lose Your Will to Live)

✓ Phone menus that never let you speak to a human.

✓ "Your call is important to us" (is it though?).

✓ The chatbot that doesn't understand anything.

✓ Shops that have 25 checkout lanes but only 2 open.

(Solution: Fake an emergency or just accept that you'll never escape hold music.)

8. Grocery Store Checkout Nightmare

✓ People who only start looking for their wallet AFTER everything is scanned.

✓ The self-checkout that says "Unexpected item in bagging area" when all you did was breathe.

✓ The cashier asking, "Do you want a bag?" when you're clearly juggling 18 loose items like a circus act.

✓ People who stand too close behind you in the queue.

The One-Person Supermarket Hold-Up

You can spot it from three checkouts away:

✓ A customer who has somehow turned a simple transaction into a full-on debate.

✓ They're discussing discounts, price checks, or complaining about a 'Buy One, Get One Free' offer from 2017.

✓ They won't leave until justice is served.

Granny's Gripes

Meanwhile, the queue behind them has started forming friendships, growing old together, and contemplating their own mortality.

The Checkout Line Jumper (AKA The Ultimate Villain)

Nothing fills me with instant rage like someone pretending not to see the queue and sneaking ahead.

✓ They 'accidentally' merge into the line.

✓ They act like it's an honest mistake.

✓ They avoid eye contact.

Yet if I shove them aside, suddenly I'm the bad guy?

The Grand Finale: The Receipt Hand-Off

Finally, the ordeal is over.

✓ I have survived.

✓ I have my groceries.

✓ I am free.

But wait! The cashier hands me a receipt that's about a metre long. Am I being handed a financial novel? A legal document? A treasure map?

Just let me leave.

(Solution: Home delivery…but then you risk getting substituted items.)

…and from Twitter:

- **English Country Life** – What grinds my gears is the person who takes ages to pay, rummaging for 5 minutes trying to find their purse in an enormous bag, then their club card, then looking for a voucher, then finding the right payment card, can't remember their PIN…they've been queuing for ten minutes!

- **Stephen Killick** – Thinking about the person who has finally packed all their purchases, only for them (usually women) to slowly go through their purse and produce numerous paper discount vouchers that all need entering individually.

- **Stephen Killick** – Food without barcodes, barcodes that are hidden, and worse, barcodes that don't work, leaving the checkout operator to find it, enter it, or, nightmare scenario, find someone to replace the damn thing, as the queue builds up behind.

- **Stephen Killick** – Back in the days when you could still locate a post office, I'd pop in for a book of stamps and invariably find myself behind someone cashing in $35 in small change.

9. Driving & Traffic Crimes (Why Are People Like This?)

✓ Drivers who pull out in front of you... and then go 10 km under the speed limit.

✓ People who don't indicate and expect you to read their minds.

✓ The 'fast lane' driver doing 15 km below the limit.

✓ The roundabout hesitation crew, GO OR DON'T, BUT MAKE A DECISION!

(Solution: Public transport... except that comes with its own list of grumbles.)

10. Public Transport Tribulations (No, That Seat Isn't Reserved for Your Bag)

✓ The one guy blasting his music on speakerphone.

✓ People who block the train doors but don't get off.

✓ The sniffly person next to you who refuses to carry tissues.

✓ People who talk on speakerphone like we all care about their conversation.

Granny's Gripes

(Solution: Noise-cancelling headphones and a strong sense of resignation.)

11. The Parking Lot Hunger Games

Shopping centre parking isn't convenience, it's a full-contact sport.

✓ You spot a park.

✓ You move in.

✓ A stealthy ninja in a hatchback steals it.

Cue the classic battles:

- **The "I Saw It First" Standoff:** Glaring. Ignoring indicators. A slow, silent war.
- **The Reverse Ambush:** One car backs out, and suddenly it's the Indy 500 with bonus shopping trolleys.
- **The Fake-Out:** Someone reaches their car... and just sits there, texting like it's a café.

My coping strategies?

✓ Park kilometres away and call it "fitness."

✓ Fantasise about online shopping forever.

12. The Slow Walker in the Middle of the Footpath

Walking should be simple. But no.

✓ Some people treat the footpath like a Sunday afternoon stroll, during peak hour.

✓ They take up the entire walkway.

✓ They move at the speed of a confused tortoise.

My advice? Either walk with purpose or get out of the way.

Final Thought: Why Do We Do This to Ourselves?

Commuting is supposed to be about getting from one place to another.

Instead, it's a daily battle against bad drivers, clueless pedestrians, and train delays that defy logic.

Honestly? Sometimes I think I should just stay home. But then, where's the fun in that?

13. The Temperature Control Struggle (Why Am I Always Too Hot or Too Cold?)

✓ Air conditioning in offices set to 'Arctic Tundra.'

✓ The weather app says 22°C. Reality: Anything but.

✓ Trying to find a comfortable doona temperature (one leg out, one leg in, full chaos).

✓ Supermarket freezers turning you into an icicle in summer.

(Solution: Layers. And rage.)

14. The Passive-Aggressive Weather (The Forecast Says One Thing, Reality Says Another)

✓ The day you don't take a coat, it rains.

✓ The day you bring an umbrella, it never rains.

✓ Leaving the house in 15°C and coming home in 32°C.

✓ Wearing the wrong shoes and regretting everything.

(Solution: Just accept that the weather is out to get you.)

15. Packaging Crimes & The War on Opening Things

✓ Plastic clamshell packaging that requires an industrial saw to open.

✓ Tiny sauce packets that explode all over you.

✓ Milk cartons that splash even when you're careful.

Granny's Gripes

✓ 'Tear here' instructions that do nothing.

(Solution: Always have scissors. And a towel for the inevitable spill.)

16. The Rise of Clamshell Packaging: A Dark Time in History

At some point, a deeply disturbed individual sat in a boardroom and said:

"What if we made packaging completely impossible to open?"

And some other lunatic replied:

"Genius! Let's encase every product in a plastic tomb of despair!"

And thus, the dark era of clamshell packaging was born.

✓ Small product? Sealed in a thick, unbreakable plastic prison.

✓ 'Easy-open' tab? A vicious lie.

✓ The edges? Sharper than a samurai sword.

It was a crime against humanity.

I would like to formally propose a ban on clamshell packaging and a return to the glorious era of sensible cardboard boxes.

✓ Easy to open.

✓ Recyclable.

✓ No risk of stabbing yourself in the hand.

Just. Use. A. Box.

17. The Plastic Waste Crime Scene

Not only is clamshell packaging a personal attack on our patience, but it's also a crime against the environment.

✓ Cardboard? Recyclable.

✓ Paper? Recyclable.

✓ Clamshell packaging? Straight to landfill, where it will outlive us all.

So, let me get this straight...

I'm buying a tiny USB stick, and it's wrapped in an unopenable plastic sarcophagus that'll still be here when the sun explodes?

...and from Twitter:

- **Stephen Killick:** In the UK, try manually accessing the bacon rashers in a Tesco pack, unless one has a sharp knife to hand.
- **Jenny Mortimer:** For me, the biggest thing is the blister pill packs, such as paracetamol. The foil on the back is industrial strength and the top is thin. I can't push the pill through! Make it make sense.

The Shopping Experience Has Been Ruined

Remember when you could get home, open your purchase, and enjoy it immediately? Now?

✓ You need scissors, a knife, and possibly a small blowtorch.

✓ You need at least 10 minutes of battle time.

✓ You need a recovery period afterwards.

Shopping used to be fun.

Now? It's a dangerous sport.

Seven (7) Restaurant & Café Grumbles

✓ The table wiper who sloshes crumbs onto your seat as you sit down.

✓ The 'rustic' restaurant lighting so dim you need a torch to read the menu.

✓ Lukewarm coffee (Coffee should be hot enough to remove the roof of your mouth, thanks.)

Granny's Gripes

✓ Restaurants that serve chips in tiny metal buckets instead of just on the damn plate.

✓ The one person who loudly recites the menu before ordering.

(Solution: Carry emergency snacks and accept your fate.)

2. The Laptop Campers – AKA the Coffee Squatters

Somewhere along the way, cafés turned into unofficial coworking spaces.

✓ One person.

✓ One laptop.

✓ One coffee… that they sip for FOUR HOURS.

Meanwhile, I just want a seat to drink my cappuccino in peace.

Listen, I get it.

Work needs to be done.

Deadlines exist.

But this isn't your office.

Either order another coffee or clear the table.

(Solution: A 'time limit' alarm that plays obnoxious music when you've overstayed your welcome.)

3. The 'Brunch Photoshoot' Crew (AKA JUST EAT YOUR FOOD!)

The waiter brings out a beautiful dish.

Hot, fresh, perfectly plated.

But does anyone eat it?

NO.

Because the 'influencers' at the next table are now holding a full production meeting about the best lighting angles.

✓ One person lifts the plate dramatically into the sunlight.

✓ Another holds their phone 5 centimetres above the eggs, whispering, "Omg, aesthetic."

✓ Someone else films a slow-motion fork-poke into a yolk, as if it's a cinematic masterpiece.

Meanwhile, I'm over here, HUNGRY, just wanting to eat my damn food.

And by the time they finally put the phone down?

The food is cold.

I hope it was worth the 17 likes on Instagram.

(Solution: A 'No Photos' section where meals must be eaten IMMEDIATELY, as nature intended.)

4. The Minimum Spend Controversy

I used to think minimum spend rules were ridiculous.

Now?

I fully support them.

✓ Sick of people nursing a single coffee for 5 hours while others need a table.

✓ Sick of 'creative meetings' that involve NO actual spending.

✓ Sick of laptop zombies treating cafés like a free workspace.

I want to eat my meal in peace.

I do not want to listen to your conference call, Karen.

Either spend more or take it elsewhere.

(Solution: If you want office space, PAY FOR ONE. Cafés are for coffee, not conference calls.)

5. The 'Food Served on Random Objects' Outrage

Granny's Gripes

Once upon a time, food came on PLATES.

Simple. Functional. Reliable.

Now?

We're getting served meals on:

✓ Wooden boards (Why? Do we look like medieval knights?)

✓ Mini shopping trolleys (WHAT IS THIS?)

✓ Slabs of rock (Did I order a steak or an archaeological dig?)

✓ Plant pots (I just wanted soup, not to feel like I'm repotting a fern.)

Just give me a bloody plate.

(Solution: A campaign for "Plates, Not Gimmicks." Who's signing the petition?)

6. The Open Kitchen Trend: A Double-Edged Sword

Ooooh, an open kitchen! You can see the chefs at work!

Sounds exciting, right? WRONG.

✓ I now have front-row seats to Gordon Ramsay-level kitchen chaos.

✓ I can hear every dropped pan, every shouted order, and every chef meltdown.

✓ I know exactly how much sweat is going into my pasta.

I didn't ask for live theatre.

I just wanted dinner.

Mystery is part of the dining experience. Close the kitchen. Let me eat in blissful ignorance.

(Solution: Open kitchens are fine... IF they come with soundproof glass.)

7. The One Person Who Takes 10 Years to Order

Christine Smith

This is a café, not an audition for MasterChef.

Yet there's always ONE person who must:

✓ Ask about every menu item.

✓ Question the origin of the coffee beans.

✓ Debate whether oat milk or almond milk is the 'right choice.'

JUST ORDER.

It's a coffee, not a life-changing decision.

(Solution: A "2-Minute Order Rule", if you take too long, you get served whatever the chef feels like.)

…and my Twitter friends chimed in:

- **Jenny Mortimer:** Meals served on a wooden platter, especially with gravy/jus/sauce.

Final Thought: Life Is a Series of Small, Unnecessary Struggles.

None of these things are major problems…

But they all add up until one day, you snap because your teabag string fell into the cup AGAIN.

That's when you realise… maybe it was never about the teabag.

Chapter 20:
Retirement – Tea, Crime & Living My Best Life

(Or: "The Best Years of My Life Are Sponsored by Tea and Homicide.")

Once upon a time, I cared about emails, staff wages, quarterly reports, and what to feed the masses each week.

Now?

✓ My biggest decision is which crime drama to watch.

✓ My schedule revolves around the kettle.

✓ The only murder mystery I care about is why I didn't retire sooner.

This, my friends, is the dream.

1. The Perfect Afternoon

🍵 Yorkshire tea.

🐈 Milo snoring.

📺 A fresh corpse in the vicarage.

No emails. No meetings. No traffic.

Just me, the cosy blanket my mum made me, and a highly suspicious local baker.

2. British Crime Dramas: Self-Care for the Soul

✓ Damp weather.

✓ Wax jackets.

✓ Awkward silences over sponge cake.

Cue brooding detectives and dramatic glances across foggy fields.

This is my therapy.

3. European Noir: Murder, But Make It Scenic

✓ Sweeping Alpine views.

✓ Haunting cello soundtracks.

✓ Expensive, frowning knitwear.

I might not understand every word, but I understand the vibe:

They're cold and underpaid.

I'm warm, retired, and debating whether to have a biscuit.

4. Exercise: Staying Upright and Fabulous

Of course, a bit of movement is critical too.

✓ Chair yoga, because honestly, who can get off the floor anymore?

✓ Gentle classes to keep me agile enough for travel (and chasing Milo).

Balance matters, especially before the wine is opened.

5. True Stories & Women Who've Had Enough

When I need inspiration, I turn to:

✓ Made in Dagenham.

✓ Hidden Figures.

✓ Anything where women fix the world while men look confused.

Cue me, clapping in the living room while Milo judges me.

6. Bridget Jones: Always the Right Answer

Sometimes, you don't need murder or revolution.

You need Bridget.

✓ Big pants.

Granny's Gripes

✓ Awkward romance.

✓ Colin Firth.

If there's no new Bridget movie soon, I will riot (peacefully, with tea).

7. The Bridget-to-Broadchurch Pipeline

One day: Colin Firth in a lake.

Next day: David Tennant brooding by the sea.

Both valid. Both retirement goals.

8. Milo at the Movies: Reviews You Didn't Ask For

- **Broadchurch** – 4/5 paws (no fish).
- **Shetland** – 5/5 paws (cosy murder approved).
- **Anything with fish** – 6/5 paws (personal bias).

Adventures Near and Far

Retirement means more than tea and TV:

✓ Travelling across the world.

✓ Visiting friends interstate.

✓ Finding the next great coffee (and a few bargains).

Freedom tastes like Yorkshire tea with a side of plane tickets.

Final Thought: Retirement Is Bliss

If you asked me whether I miss work, I'd laugh until I spilled my tea.

Retirement =

✓ Tea on tap.

✓ Murder without consequences.

✓ Chair yoga and no alarms.

And honestly? I'm content.

"My life is now 80% tea, 10% murder mysteries, 10% chair yoga, the best health plan I've ever had."

Final Thought: A Toast to Friendship (And the People Who Keep Us Honest)

Good Mates, Bad Jokes & A Lifetime of Banter

Sheila from the Antipodes: A Tribute to Ian and the Art of Banter

Everyone has that one friend who simultaneously annoys and delights you in equal measure. Mine happens to be a retired naval officer, let's call him Ian ("no names, no pack drill," as they say in the services).

Ian refuses to acknowledge my Yorkshire roots. No matter how many times I remind him that I'm a Pom through and through, he insists on introducing me as:

"This is Sheila from the Antipodes."

The first time, it was funny. The hundredth? Well, it's still funny, but don't tell him that.

Whether it's pub quiz night or Christmas morning at church, Ian never misses a chance to remind me (and everyone within earshot) that I now hail from Down Under.

Case in point:

One Christmas, I agreed to attend church with Ian and my longest-known friend, Alyson (his far more sensible wife). After the service, when leaving, Ian turned to the vicar and, with a completely straight face, declared:

"This is Sheila from Australia. She had to use her passport to get in here this morning."

To be fair, he wasn't entirely wrong. Because of security at the naval dockyard, I did have to show my Australian passport just to get into church. Apparently, I'm not just from the Antipodes, I'm an alien.

But why do I put up with Ian?

✓ Because good friends are hard to come by.

Granny's Gripes

✓ Because he gives me a reason to sharpen my wit regularly.

✓ Because he appreciates a woman who can hold her own with a glass of red wine.

✓ And because, at the end of the day, we share a camaraderie that only true friends have.

He calls me Sheila.

I call him Shipmate, a title of respect and endearment in the Royal Navy.

And no matter how many times I correct him, I know he'll never stop calling me Sheila. And honestly? I wouldn't have it any other way.

Would he immediately find a way to one-up me next time we meet? Without a doubt. But that's what good friendships are made of.

Folks, a reminder that despite all the grumbles, sarcasm, and everyday irritations, the best parts of life are the people we share it with.

Appendix:

A Viewing Plan for Every Retirement Mood (weirdly useful)

Mood	Recommendation
Need Comfort	*Bridget Jones, Calendar Girls, The Best Exotic Marigold Hotel*
Need to Feel Powerful	*Made in Dagenham, Hidden Figures, Erin Brockovich*
Need to See Men Suffer in Knitwear	*Broadchurch, Shetland, The Killing*
Need Scenic Deaths	*The Bridge, Trapped, Wallander*

Handy Guide 1: The Official Tea-Flake Accountability Guide

(Or: "How to Prosecute Those Who Dare to Stand Up a Brew")

Section 1: The Crime – Abandoning a Cuppa Without Cause

A Tea-Flake is defined as:

✓ Someone who enthusiastically agrees to pop round for tea… then fails to show up.

✓ A person who claims to love tea but has no respect for the sacred ritual.

✓ A repeat offender who routinely ghosts afternoon tea like a bad Tinder date.

These people must be stopped.

Section 2: Acceptable Excuses for Missing Tea (A Very Short List)

◊ Kidnapped by aliens. *(Must provide photographic evidence.)*

◊ Sudden, unavoidable fame. *(If whisked away to Hollywood, we'll allow it, but only if you take us to the Oscars.)*

Granny's Gripes

- ◇ Accidental time travel. *(But be warned, you still owe us tea in both timelines.)*

- ◇ A Milo-related emergency. *(If the cat is involved, we understand. For now.)*

If your excuse is "I got busy" or "I forgot," prepare to face The Tea Tribunal.

Section 3: Punishments for Tea-Flakes

- **First Offence:** *The Stern Look of Disappointment.*

  You will receive a formally issued glare that can curdle milk.

- **Second Offence:** *Public Shaming.*

  ✓ Named and shamed at the next gathering.

  ✓ Expect to hear, "Oh look, it's Her Majesty the Tea-Flake!" whenever you enter a room.

- **Third Offence:** *Biscuit Privileges Revoked.*

  ✓ No biscuits for you, not even the broken ones at the bottom of the tin.

- **Fourth Offence:** *Forced Instant Coffee Sentence.*

  ✓ Your next cuppa will be instant coffee from a dodgy office breakroom.

  ✓ No milk. No sugar. Served lukewarm in a chipped mug with an inspirational quote.

- **Fifth Offence:** *Blacklisted from Tea Society.*

  ✓ Barred from all future tea-related invitations.

  ✓ Name placed on the National Tea-Flake Watchlist.

  ✓ Kettle rights suspended indefinitely.

Section 4: Redemption for Tea-Flakes

To regain trust, an offender must complete one of the following tasks:

✓ Host a tea gathering *(with homemade scones as an act of penance)*.

✓ Supply top-tier biscuits for three consecutive tea sessions.

✓ Make a public apology *(extra points if performed in Shakespearean monologue style)*.

✓ Buy tea in bulk for the next meet-up *(Earl Grey, Yorkshire Gold, or Darjeeling, no Lipton swill)*.

Once the Tea Tribunal has deemed the offender rehabilitated, they may resume their place in polite society.

Final Note: The Sacredness of Tea

A good cuppa isn't just a drink, it's a contract of trust. A moment of peace, comfort, and human connection. To disrespect it is to disrespect the very fabric of civilisation.

So let's be clear:

☕ You don't ghost a cuppa.

☕ You don't abandon a teapot

☕ You **do** show up, sit down, and enjoy your bloody tea.

If not? Prepare for judgement.

Handy Guide 2: Enjoying Retirement (Without Becoming Boring)

✓ **Move!** *(Not just from bed to couch, actual movement. Even if it's just aggressively rearranging the pantry.)*

✓ **Use your brain.** *(Read. Write. Solve a murder mystery in your head. Just don't become the person who shares weird Facebook chain posts.)*

Granny's Gripes

✓ **Stay social.** *(But only with people you like. Life's too short for dull conversations about knee replacements.)*

✓ **Try something new.** *(Not saying you need to take up skydiving, but even swapping brands of tea counts as adventure.)*

✓ **Make peace with naps.** *(You've earned them. Just don't let them turn into full-on hibernation.)*

Handy Guide 3: Navigating Small Talk Without Losing Your Will to Live

✓ **Step 1:** Default to the weather. *(Dull but effective. Just don't become a meteorologist mid-conversation.)*

✓ **Step 2:** Ask them about themselves. *(Most people love talking about themselves. Let them entertain you while you sip your drink.)*

✓ **Step 3:** Find a polite exit. *("Well, I won't keep you!" = the social equivalent of a parachute.)*

✓ **Step 4:** Fake an emergency if needed. *(Sudden need for the loo? Long-lost phone call? Whatever gets you out cleanly.)*

✓ **Step 5:** If stuck, mention an obscure historical fact. *(Most people will back away slowly to avoid further conversation.)*

Handy Guide 4: Handling Modern Tech Without Throwing It Out the Window

✓ **Rule 1:** When in doubt, turn it off and on again. *(90% of IT help desks are built on this wisdom.)*

✓ **Rule 2:** Updates will ruin everything. *(One day your apps work. The next, your banking app needs a face scan, your emails vanish, and your phone now thinks you live in Uzbekistan.)*

✓ **Rule 3:** Passwords are out to get you. *(No, you can't use "password123" anymore. But you also can't remember the ultra-secure one your phone insisted on creating.)*

✓ **Rule 4:** Autocorrect is your enemy. *(You said, "nice meeting", not "nude meeting." Good luck explaining that one.)*

✓ **Rule 5:** If all else fails, find a child. *(They'll fix it in 10 seconds, roll their eyes, and call you old. Accept your fate.)*

Handy Guide 5: Surviving the Grocery Store Checkout (Without a Criminal Record)

✓ **Tactic 1:** Scan the queues early. *(Looks short? Don't be fooled. The person in front will pay with a bag of coins and a complicated coupon system.)*

✓ **Tactic 2:** Self-checkout is a trap. *(It will accuse you of stealing at least once. It thrives on suspicion.)*

✓ **Tactic 3:** Beware the Chatty Cashier. *(You're not their therapist. You just want your groceries and your sanity intact.)*

✓ **Tactic 4:** Pay attention to the person in front. *(Are they pulling out a cheque book? Abandon ship immediately.)*

✓ **Tactic 5:** If all else fails, order online. *(Let someone else deal with the checkout drama.)*

Handy Guide 6: Spotting a Manspreader in the Wild (and How to Handle It)

✓ **Stage 1:** Spot the manspreader. *(Legs at a 90-degree angle? Arms claiming both armrests? You've found one.)*

✓ **Stage 2:** The Subtle Nudge. *(Accidental bag placement or a gentle knee nudge. See if they get the hint.)*

✓ **Stage 3:** The Direct Approach. *("Excuse me, sir, but are you trying to birth a watermelon?")*

✓ **Stage 4:** If All Else Fails, Go Full Chaos. *(Dramatically spread your own legs. Knock over your coffee. Make it weird for everyone.)*

✓ **Stage 5:** Document & Share. *(Bonus points if you caption it: "Live footage of someone taking up space like they own the planet.")*

Handy Guide 7: Grumpy Party Games – Elevating Awkward Social Situations with Structured Grumpiness

Guess the Passive-Aggressive Comment: Players take turns saying phrases that seem polite but drip with sarcasm. Example: "Oh, your casserole is so…creative!" Points awarded for spotting the subtle shade.

Pin the Blame on the Scapegoat: Blindfolded, you must pin the blame for hypothetical disasters on a cardboard cutout of, say, your boss or the family member most likely to leave dishes in the sink. Bonus points for creative finger-pointing.

Eye-Roll Bingo: Each player gets a bingo card filled with classic eye-roll triggers: "Someone overshares about their keto diet," "The printer jams," or "Aunt Linda brings up politics." First to complete a row wins *half-hearted applause*.

The Grumpy Trivia Challenge: Questions include gems like: "What's the longest line at the DMV ever recorded?" or "How many seconds into a call does tech support recommend turning it off and on again?" Winners earn bragging rights and an extra slice of pie.

Social etiquette might be a maze, but with these tips, you'll survive, and even enjoy, the chaos of human interaction.

Sign Off

Keep Rolling Those Eyes – It's Good for You

Well, here we are.

You've made it to the end, and honestly, that deserves a biscuit and a proper cup of tea.

But before you toddle off to do something more useful *(like alphabetise the spice rack or argue with the cat)*, here's the thing:

This book isn't really finished. Not if you've still got stories to share, giggles to spread, and a healthy disdain for the ridiculous.

Christine Smith

So what now?

✓ Share your own everyday irritations, the world needs more good gripes.

✓ Laugh *(loudly)* in the face of nonsense.

✓ Join me and a merry band of fellow eye-rollers in my Facebook group: https://bit.ly/3X87cgP Granny Gripes *(it's not just for grandmas, or grumpy people, really).*

✓ Or drop me a line, I do love a good story, especially the ones that start with, "You won't believe what just happened…"

Because honestly?

Life's too short to stay silent when there's so much madness to gently mock.

So keep rolling your eyes, keep laughing at the chaos, and keep finding the fun where you can. It's the only sensible response to the world most days.

And if all else fails, remember: **Tea first. Sarcasm second. Pants optional.**

Stay in touch:

✓ **Instagram:** @TheFoodGranny

✓ **Facebook Group:** https://bit.ly/3X87cgP

✓ **Email:** grannygripes1@gmail.com

✓ **Substack:** Forks to Footprints *(Subscribe, it's FREE, for more real-life rantings and rambles.)*

"The world may be mad, but at least we've got tea and sarcasm."

Author's Note

If this book made you laugh, sigh, or mutter "oh, for heaven's sake," then my work here is done.

Thanks for reading and remember:

Life's ridiculous. You might as well enjoy it.

(And don't forget to put the kettle on.)

www.ingramcontent.com/pod-product-compliance
Lightning Source LLC
Chambersburg PA
CBHW071217070526
44584CB00019B/3058